Hitting THE BOOKS

Skills for Reading, Writing, and Research

Science

Projects

Meg Greve

Rourke

Educational Media

rourkeeducationalmedia.com

Before Reading:

Building Academic Vocabulary and Background Knowledge

Before reading a book, it is important to tap into what your child or students already know about the topic. This will help them develop their vocabulary, increase their reading comprehension, and make connections across the curriculum.

1. *Look at the cover of the book. What will this book be about?*
2. *What do you already know about the topic?*
3. *Let's study the Table of Contents. What will you learn about in the book's chapters?*
4. *What would you like to learn about this topic? Do you think you might learn about it from this book? Why or why not?*
5. *Use a reading journal to write about your knowledge of this topic. Record what you already know about the topic and what you hope to learn about the topic.*
6. *Read the book.*
7. *In your reading journal, record what you learned about the topic and your response to the book.*
8. *After reading the book complete the activities below.*

Content Area Vocabulary
Read the list. What do these words mean?

citation
complex
controls
experts
field
hypothesis
observations
outcome
research
variables

After Reading:

Comprehension and Extension Activity

After reading the book, work on the following questions with your child or students in order to check their level of reading comprehension and content mastery.

1. *Why is it important to test only one variable at a time in a science experiment? (Asking Questions)*
2. *How might you go about picking a topic for a science project? (Visualize)*
3. *What are you looking for when testing variables in a science project? (Infer)*
4. *List the different steps of a science project. (Summarize)*
5. *Why is it important to pick a topic or field you are interested in? (Text to self connection)*

Extension Activity

After reading the book, conduct a science experiment at home with a friend. Find a topic that interests you both and follow the steps outlined in the book to see if your experiment turned out the way you thought it would. Share your thoughts with your friend and see what their expected outcome was. Was it the same as yours? Was it different? If so, explain how.

Table of Contents

What Do You Wonder? 4

The Process 12

Testing, Testing 17

The Outcome 20

Glossary 22

Index 23

Websites to Visit 23

About the Author 24

What Do You Wonder?

Have you ever wondered about the world around you? Maybe you've asked yourself if certain colors attract bees or if one brand of toothpaste is really better than another. Perhaps you've wondered if there's a better way to mow your front lawn. If you ask yourself questions like these, you may have the makings of a great scientific experiment!

Scientific experiments can be as simple as growing a seed under different conditions, or as **complex** as designing a new way to power a rocket into space. Science projects can answer questions you have about the world. The key is to ask yourself, "What do I wonder?"

Project Tip

Keep and carry a small notebook or make notes on an electronic device. As you go about your daily life, write down questions or **observations** you have about the world. As you read through your notes, you may be surprised to find that you have already developed a great science experiment idea.

A science experiment has been assigned in class, and you are probably feeling overwhelmed. What will your topic be? What is your question? Don't worry. Paying attention to the things you wonder about is the best way to choose a topic or idea. Choose a question or **field** in which you are interested. Science projects will feel less overwhelming when you truly want to know the answer.

Write down as many questions as you can about interesting topics. Pay attention to science events you hear about in the news. Watch commercials on television. Are they making claims you think may not be true? Once you have some questions, start narrowing down your choices. Then choose one question you really want to answer.

- How does mold grow?
- Do plants need water?
- Are dogs colorblind?
- Why do apples turn brown?

Once you have chosen a question, your next step is to learn as much as you can about the topic. Say your question is, "Under what conditions will a seed grow best?" Your next step would be to **research** plant growth and seeds. Use your library and the Internet to learn all you can about the topic. Be sure to take detailed notes. Your science project will also include a research paper.

When conducting research, begin reading each text carefully. Write down what you have learned in your own words. Write down any new questions that occur to you as you read. Circle these questions so you remember to look for the answers as you continue your research.

Make note of the title of the book or website and all of the important **citation** information. You will need this later when you are writing your paper.

Research is not just reading books and website information. You should also talk to **experts** in the field you are researching. For a plant experiment, you might visit a garden center. Find someone interested in talking to you about your science experiment. Experts will have a great deal of knowledge to share with you. They may even have some advice on the best way to conduct your experiment.

Create a page with questions you have about the topic. Include questions you came up with during your research. Be prepared when you talk with an expert. He or she will not have a lot of time to spend with you, so you want to use your time well.

Talking with an expert will help you further understand your topic and be better prepared to conduct your research.

The Process

Now that you have learned all you can about your topic, it is time to create your **hypothesis**. You should write your hypothesis, or prediction, in such a way that it will give you something to test. The best way to do this is to write an if/then statement. For example: "If I _____, then _____will happen."

Project Tip

Your hypothesis must be something that can be tested. The hypothesis is the basis for the science experiment. If it cannot be tested, you may have to change your question or hypothesis.

If water is hot, then salt will dissolve quicker.

Most science experiments include **variables** and **controls**. To make sure your test is fair, you must be sure to test only one variable at a time. For example, if you are testing which temperature water is best to dissolve salt, you would change only the temperature of the water. The rest of the materials stay the same for each trial. You use the same amount of salt, the same amount of water, the same size and type of container, and even the same amount of stirs in the water.

Changing the water temperature to test your hypothesis is the most important variable in your experiment, so be sure that you are writing everything down and keeping good notes.

You are testing to find the **outcome** when that one variable is changed. Once you choose your variable, it is time to start planning and writing your experiment.

Testing, Testing

The fun part is about to start! When planning and writing your experiment, think of it as a recipe. List all the materials you will need, the amount of time the experiment will take, any safety rules, and a step-by-step list of how you will conduct the experiment. Your steps should be so clear that anyone can follow them and get the same outcome.

Materials needed:
1. salt
2. tablespoon
3. 3 cups of the same size
4. water
5. notebook
6. pen

17

When you begin to test, write down everything you do and what happens. If you have to change a step or the amount of a material, be sure to make a note. Follow science safety procedures by wearing goggles when necessary and getting adult supervision.

Procedure

1. Fill cup #1 with cold water from the refrigerator and add two heaping tablespoons of salt.
2. Stir with spoon until salt dissolves making sure to keep an eye on the time.
3. Record results.
4. Fill cup #2 with room temperature water from the faucet and add two heaping tablespoons of salt.
5. Stir with spoon until salt dissolves making sure to keep an eye on the time.
6. Record results.
7. Fill cup #3 with boiling water and add two heaping tablespoons of salt.
8. Stir with spoon until salt dissolves making sure to keep an eye on the time.
9. Record results.

Project Tip

How will you record the results of your test? Will you draw pictures, write in a table, or create a graph? It is a good idea to take pictures as you conduct your experiment. You can use these when presenting your project.

Filling cup #2 with room temperature water

Pouring 2 tbsp. of salt into cup #2

The Outcome

Once you have conducted your test more than once, look at your results. Was your hypothesis correct? Sometimes a hypothesis is not correct. This does not mean your experiment failed. It means you have learned something new. Discovering your outcome might lead to a new question you have about your topic and give you another chance to continue learning all you can through more research and experiments. Write down your findings and get ready to share them.

Presentation Board

| Problem | Does water temperature affect the time it takes for salt to dissolve in liquid? | Results |

Hypothesis

Procedure   Variables

Materials   Conclusion

Sharing what you learned allows you to celebrate your hard work. Share your work on a presentation board. Be sure to make your presentation neat, spell correctly, and include all parts of your experiment. If you are presenting to a group, practice your speech and use note cards to write down important facts.

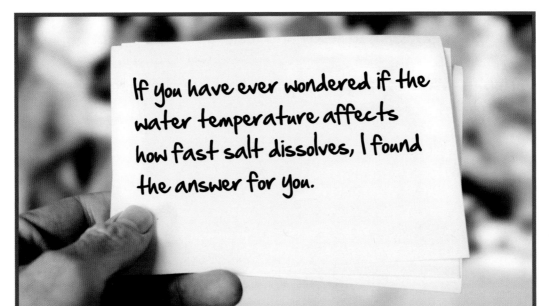

If you have ever wondered if the water temperature affects how fast salt dissolves, I found the answer for you.

Glossary

citation (sie-TAY-shuhn): explanation of where information was gathered including the title of the work, author, and date of publication

complex (KOM-plex): complicated and not simple

controls (kuhn-TROHLS): things that do not change

experts (EK-spurts): people who have the most knowledge about a certain topic

field (FEELD): area of study

hypothesis (hye-POTH-uh-siss): a prediction or guess that can be tested in an experiment

observations (ob-zur-VAY-shuhns): things you have noticed about something

outcome (OUT-kuhm): the result

research (ri-SURCH): to study and learn about a subject

variables (VAIR-ee-uh-buhls): things that are changed or kept the same in an experiment

Index

experiment 4, 6, 10, 13, 17, 19, 20, 21

notes 5, 9

outcome 16, 17, 20

prediction 12

presentation 21

question(s) 4, 6, 7, 9, 11, 20

research 9, 10, 11, 20

safety 17, 18

topic(s) 6, 7, 9, 11, 12, 20

Websites  to Visit

http://www.sciencebob.com/experiments/index.php

http://www.sciencebuddies.org/

http://spaceplace.nasa.gov/science-fair/en/

About the Author

Meg Greve lives in Chicago with her husband Tom, and her two children, Madison and William. William loves to do science experiments. The messier, the better!

Meet The Author!
www.meetREMauthors.com

www.rourkeeducationalmedia.com

PHOTO CREDITS: Cover © JBryson, Kaliq; title page © Sergii Moskaliuk, Monkey Business Images; page 3 © Dwafotografy; page 4 © kwaipun; page 5 © YUNUS ARAKON; page 6, 16 © Wavebreak Media LTD; page 7 © everthing possible; page 8, 11 © Dragon Images; page 9 © Chalong Tawan; page 10 © JBryson; page 12 © HONGQI ZHANG; page 13, 19 © Sergil Moskaliuk, Viorel Sima; page 14, 19 © Mario Bonotto; page 15 © goodluz; page 17 © Diana Valujeva; page 18 © Ivan Danik; page 19 © Elena Elisseeva; page 20 © Moonboard; page 21 © Bar Rafaeli

Edited by: Jill Sherman

Cover and Interior Design by: Jen Thomas

Library of Congress PCN Data

Science Projects / Meg Greve
(Hitting the Books: Skills for Reading, Writing, and Research)
ISBN (hard cover) 978-1-62717-690-3 (alk. paper)
ISBN (soft cover) 978-1-62717-812-9
ISBN (e-Book) 978-1-62717-927-0
Library of Congress Control Number: 2014935484

Rourke Educational Media
Printed in the United States of America,
North Mankato, Minnesota

Also Available as: